Daniel Fast Cookbook Beginners-Over 50 Daniel Fast Recipes for Breakfast, Lunch, Dinner, Snacks, Slow Cooker, Smoothies and Desserts

by Debbie Madson, Madson Web Publishing, LLC

Specialty Cooking Series

The Daniel Fast diet is a spiritual fast, based on the principle of drawing closer to God through a disciplined eating plan combined with prayer. The aim of the fast is not merely to improve your eating habits, but also to enhance and strengthen your spiritual connection to God.
I especially love it for its simple and healthy eating plan.

Table of Contents

What is the Daniel Fast Diet?

The Daniel Fast diet is a spiritual fast, based on the principle of drawing closer to God through a disciplined eating plan combined with prayer. The aim of the fast is not merely to improve your eating habits, but also to enhance and strengthen your spiritual connection to God. It helps to start the Daniel Fast with a specific question or purpose, so you can contemplate this challenge during the fast.

History of the Daniel Fast

The Fast is inspired by the events narrated in the Bible chapter of Daniel. In the First Book of Daniel, the Prophet Daniel ate only vegetables and drank only water for 10 days. In the 10th book of Daniel, he went on a second 3-week fast, when he "ate no pleasant food, no meat and no wine." This second fast specifically mentions avoiding sweeteners, leavened bread and wine.

Daniel and his three friends had been taken to Babylon where they were commanded to observe Babylonian custom. However, this involved eating meat, so Daniel asked if he could be excused from eating meat.

The Bible does not command Christians to fast, so the Daniel fast is seen as a voluntary expression of faith. Today people observe the Daniel Fast for a specific time-frame as part of a spiritual journey designed to benefit their health.

The Principles of the Daniel Fast

During the Daniel Fast, you only eat plant-based foods, such as fruit, vegetables and whole grains, and you only drink water. This way, you are using foods created by God to nourish your body, which was designed by God. Avoid sweeteners and breads, as well as artificial and processed foods.

The foods you eat during the fast have spiritual significance, based on two main Bible scriptures. In Daniel 1, Daniel ate only vegetables and drank only water. This has been modified to include fruits and vegetables. In Daniel 10, for 21 days he ate no meat nor any precious foods or breads, and drank no wine. Based on this scripture, you avoid sweeteners and breads during the Daniel Fast. The Daniel Fast also observes the Jewish fasting principles by avoiding leavening agents such as yeast or baking powder.

If you follow these three principles exactly –
only fruits, vegetables, whole grains and
water, with no bread or sweeteners – you
automatically eliminate artificial additives and
preservatives.

Prayer is another important element of the
Daniel Fast. Allocate specific times each day
for prayer and contemplation.

What foods am I permitted to eat?

During the Daniel Fast, you are limited to plant-based foods with water as your only beverage. You must also avoid deep-fried foods, sweeteners and rising agents. This might seem a limited list, but when you investigate more closely, you will see you have quite a good range of delicious and healthy foods to choose from. Always read any labels of any packaged, canned or bottled foods to ensure that all ingredients comply with the restrictions of the diet.

If you select a variety of foods from each of the following categories, you will maintain a healthy and balanced intake of nutrients throughout the Daniel Fast.

All fruits and vegetables: You can eat any kind of fruit or vegetables, whether it is fresh, frozen, dried, juiced or canned. This includes veggie burgers.

Legumes: All legumes, such as pinto beans, kidney beans, black beans or split peas, are permitted in the Daniel Fast, whether they are canned or dried.

Whole grains: The whole grain category includes whole wheat, brown rice, quinoa, oats or barley. While you cannot eat bread or anything sweetened or cooked with a raising agent, you can replace bread with whole wheat tortillas, rice cakes or whole wheat pasta.

Nuts and seeds: Keep a variety of nuts on hand, such as cashews, peanuts or almonds, as well as seeds such as sesame and canola seeds. You can also eat nut butters, but check the ingredient list carefully, to ensure it complies with the dietary restrictions. While you cannot have any beverages besides water, you can use unsweetened almond milk in recipes.

Oils: Vegetable and seed oils such as olive oil, peanut oil and sesame oil are a great supplement to the other foods on the menu.

Soy and tofu: Tofu and soy sauce are included in the Daniel Fast menu, and you can also add unsweetened soy milk to recipes, although it cannot be drunk as a beverage.

Natural flavoring: You can add some natural zestful flavor to your meals with salt, herbs and spices, or vinegar.

Citric acid: You will find this ingredient listed on some packaged foods. Citric acid is a natural preservative derived from fruits, which makes it permissible to consume during the Daniel Fast.

Pure water: Water is the only beverage permitted during the Daniel Fast. You can drink any pure water, such as spring water or distilled water or plain tap water.

What foods should I avoid?

The premise of the Daniel Fast is to consume only natural plant-based foods, without any additional sweeteners or leavened bread. But simply avoiding meat and bread is not enough. Here we look at the specific foods you must avoid during the Daniel Fast.

Meat and animal products: All meat, including beef, pork, lamb and poultry, and all fish are forbidden during the Daniel Fast. Dairy foods and eggs are also classified as animal products and must be avoided. You can replace dairy milk in cooking with almond milk, rice milk or soy milk.

Sweeteners: Avoid sugar, honey, syrup and cane juice, and do not eat any packaged food that has been sweetened.

Baked goods: Avoid leavened bread and other baked goods that contain yeast and/ or sweeteners such as honey.

Refined and processed foods: Do not consume foods made from white flour, white rice, or foods that contain artificial flavors, additives or preservatives.

Solid fats: Avoid foods containing margarine, butter or lard, and do not consume deep fried foods such as potato chips. (However, you can oven-fry potato or sweet potato for home made fries/ chips).

Beverages: The only beverage permitted during the Daniel Fast is pure water, so avoid carbonated drinks, milk, coffee tea, herbal tea

Preparing for the Daniel Fast

You need to prepare both spiritually and in a practical sense to make the most of your Daniel fast.

Find a spiritual purpose

First, you need to decide on a purpose for your fast. What are you seeking from God? Do you need strength or wisdom, or a revelation about a certain aspect of your life?

You should also establish a purpose based on someone else's needs, so you can pray that they find strength, wisdom or guidance. Is there someone close to you who is lost or struggling? You can pray on their behalf during your Daniel fast. Tell that person you will be praying for them during the fast.

Prepare your pantry

It is easier to stick with an eating plan if you have all the necessary foods on hand. Stock up on whole grains, brown rice, nuts and other important components of the fast. Plan your schedule so you are prepared to replenish your supplies of fresh fruits and vegetables every few days.

Think ahead about how you will handle social occasions, such as dinner with friends, or even lunch at work. Planning will prevent you finding yourself hungry with nothing appropriate to eat.

Plan a few balanced meals and snacks so your eating plan is completely ready to go!

Know your weaknesses

If caffeine, processed foods or sweet treats are a regular part of your daily eating plan, you will find it difficult to go "cold turkey" for the duration of your fast. Your spiritual journey may be distracted by your unhealthy cravings and mood swings.

You can circumvent this by gradually cutting down on your food dependencies in the weeks leading up to the fast: consume the forbidden items less often until you can comfortably go a full day without coffee or chocolate. This way, the Daniel Fast will be an extension of your healthy eating goals rather than an impossibly strict challenge.

See your doctor

Whenever you prepare to make drastic changes to your eating plan, make sure your doctor does a few routine tests first. Have a blood test to check your vitamin and mineral count, and ask your doctor to check your blood pressure and your glucose levels. If any of these are outside the normal range, a change in diet could aggravate the issue. For example, if your iron or Vitamin B12 levels are already low, you will become extremely lethargic when you cut meat and dairy from your daily eating plan. However, if you have all these issues checked in advance, you can tailor your diet to work around any problems. Another benefit to seeing your doctor first is that you can take a snapshot of your health before the Daniel Fast, and then see how your health has improved after the 21-day abstinence from caffeine, sugar and processed foods.

Benefits of the Daniel Fast

A diet based on fruit, vegetables, nuts and whole grains, without sugars or processed food is extremely beneficial for your health, even if you only maintain the Daniel Fast for a specific time-frame, such as 10 days or 21 days. This eating plan has been proven to improve energy levels, blood pressure, cholesterol levels, immunity, memory, indigestion and skin problems such as acne or eczema. It has also been seen to reduce chronic health issues such as headaches, depression, indigestion and bloating.

It is also a wonderful opportunity to focus on your faith and feel sustained by the strength and love of God.

Daniel Fast Breakfast Recipes

Baked Fruity Oatmeal

Serves: 4.

Ingredients:

1 Cup rolled oats
1 Tablespoon chopped pecans
2 Tablespoons chopped dried apricots
1 Cup almond milk, unsweetened
2 Tablespoons chopped or sliced bananas
1/4 Cup + 1 tablespoon baked purred apple or unsweetened apple sauce
1/2 teaspoon ground cinnamon

Directions:

Preheat oven to 180C/350F and slightly grease 6x6-inch baking pan with some olive oil. Place all listed ingredients by order in a bowl. Stir well to combine and transfer into prepared pan. Bake the prepared mixture for 40 minutes or until slightly brown on top. Set on wire rack to cool before slicing and serving. Substitute any dried fruit you prefer.

Banana Carrot Muffins

Serves: 10 muffins

Ingredients:

2 large carrots, grated

1 Cup ground oatmeal

1/2 Cup unsweetened applesauce

1 1/2 Cups mashed ripe bananas

1 Cup whole wheat flour

1 1/2 teaspoon fresh lemon juice

1/2 vanilla pod, seeds scraped out

Directions:

Preheat oven to 180C/350F and slightly grease muffin tin with olive oil.

Combine carrot, banana, vanilla seeds and lemon juice in a bowl.

In separate bowl, whisk all dry ingredients and fold into carrot mixture.

Stir until just combined and spoon the mixture into prepared muffin tin.

Bake muffins in preheated oven for 20-25 minutes or until inserted toothpick comes out clean.

Set on wire rack to cool slightly before serving.

NOTE: You can use quinoa instead oatmeal.

Tofu Scramble

Serves: 2

Ingredients:

2 red bell peppers, thinly sliced or chopped
2 green onions, finely chopped
1 box firm tofu, drained and broken into pieces
1 garlic clove, peeled and minced
1 tablespoon fresh chives, chopped
Small pinch of ground sea salt

Directions:

Spray or slightly coat large non-stick skillet
with pure olive oil.
Place all ingredients and stir using wooden
spoon.
Cook until veggies are tender, for 10 minutes
over medium heat.
Season with salt and serve.

Fruit Tortillas

Serves: 6 tortillas

Ingredients:

For the tortillas:

1 tablespoon pure olive oil

1 cup whole wheat flour

1/4 teaspoon salt

1/4 Cup warm water

For the filling:

1 1/2 cups mixed berries, crushed

1 1/2 teaspoons fresh lemon juice

Directions:

Mix flour and salt in a bowl. Add olive oil and stir until well combined. Gradually add warm water until mixture start to pull away from the sides of bowl. Transfer the dough onto floured mixture and knead around 20 times. Set the dough to rest for 15 minutes and form into log shape. Cut into 6 equal parts and using rolling pin roll out each ball to tortilla. Heat large non-stick skillet over medium-high heat and fry tortillas for 30 seconds per side. Set them aside to keep warm and prepare the fruits. Combine fruits with lemon juice and place in microwave safe dish. Heat for 20 seconds and

spread over tortillas. Wrap them up and slice in half before serving.
NOTE: You can use other fruits like nectarines, plums etc.

Fruity Quinoa

Serves: 2

Ingredients:

1/2 Cup uncooked quinoa

1/4 Cup blueberries

1/4 Cup blackberries

1/2 Cup chopped almonds

1 cup almond milk, unsweetened

Small pinch cinnamon

1 tablespoon chopped dried plums

1/2 vanilla pod, seed scraped out

Directions:

In a small sauce pan, combine almond milk, vanilla and quinoa. Bring to boil over medium high heat and reduce heat to medium-low. Simmer for 15 minutes or until milk is fully incorporated and quinoa is tender. Transfer quinoa to a serving bowls and add remaining ingredients. Stir to combine and serve while still hot.

Breakfast Oat Pancakes

Serves: 4

Ingredients:

1 Cup whole wheat flour
1/4 Cup blueberries or sliced strawberries
1 Cup unsweetened almond milk
1/4 Cup unsweetened apple sauce
Small pinch ground sea salt
Some olive oil, for frying

Directions:

In a medium sized bowl combine flour and salt. Add almond milk and apple sauce. Stir until just combined. Add fruits and stir well. Heat around 1 teaspoon of oil in non-stick pan and over medium-high heat. Drop ¼ cup of mixture onto hot pan and with swirl motions distribute the batter evenly over pan.
Cook the pancakes for 1-2 minutes per side or until bubbly and golden. Serve while still hot.

Oats and Fruit Smoothie

Serves: 2

Ingredients:

1 Cup unsweetened almond milk

1 ripe banana

1/2 Cup rolled oats

1/4 Cup raspberries or blueberries

1/4 Cup mango chunks

Directions:

Place all ingredients in food blender. Pulse until smooth. Serve immediately.

Pumpkin Waffles

Serves: 4

Ingredients:

3/4 Cup whole wheat flour

1/4 Cup almond meal

1 Cup pumpkin puree

1 1/2 Cups almond milk, unsweetened

1/4 Cup applesauce, unsweetened

2 Tablespoons cornmeal

1 teaspoon pure olive oil

Small pinch salt

1/2 teaspoon cinnamon

1/4 teaspoon nutmeg

1/2 cup water – optional add if batter seems to thick

Directions:

In a medium sized bowl, combine almond milk, apple sauce, pumpkin puree, spices, olive oil and stir well. In separate bowl, combine corn meal, flour and almond meal. Add the flours mixture into wet mixture and stir until well blended. Check the consistency and add water until you have desired batter. Heat waffle iron and pour in the batter so waffle iron is nicely filled. Cook for 3 minutes or until golden. Serve while still hot with fresh fruits.

NOTE: If want you can add tablespoon of chopped nuts for a crunchier version.

Daniel Fast Lunch recipes

Potato Soup

Serves: 4

Ingredients:

3 Cups water

1/2 teaspoon ground sea salt

4 Cups potatoes, peeled and cubed

1/2 Cup almond milk

2 garlic cloves, minced

1 teaspoon dried parsley

1 Tablespoon pure olive oil

1 Cup carrots, chopped

1 Cup celery, chopped

Small pinch black pepper

1/2 teaspoon thyme

1/2 small onion, chopped

Directions:

Heat olive oil in medium sized sauce pan over medium-high heat. Add celery, carrots and onion; cook until tender. Add garlic and cook for 1 minute further. Pour in water and add potatoes, spices and herbs. Reduce heat to medium-low, stir and simmer for 30 minutes or until potatoes are tender. Remove from the heat and transfer half of potatoes in food processor. Pulse until smooth and place in the soup. Stir in almond milk and set back over heat until heated through. Serve while still hot.

Fast Avocado Pasta

Serves: 4

Ingredients:

12 oz. whole wheat pasta

2 medium sized avocados, pitted

4 garlic cloves

1 teaspoon fresh ground sea salt

3 tablespoons pure olive oil

1 lemon juiced + zest

1/4 Cup fresh basil

Some fresh pepper

Directions:

Pour water in large pot and season with salt. Heat over high heat and when start to boil, add in pasta. Cook according to package directions. Drain pasta and set aside.

Meanwhile prepared the avocado sauce; place peeled garlic cloves, olive oil and lemon juice in food processor. Pulse until you have smooth mix. Add avocado, basil and season with salt and pepper. Process until smooth and creamy.

Transfer the sauce in pot with pasta and stir to coat pasta well.

Divide between four plates and garnish with some lemon zest before serving.

Oven Baked Mexican Bean Burgers

Serves: 4

Ingredients:

1/4 Cup whole wheat flour

8 oz. red can kidney beans, drained and mashed

1 rice cake, crushed

1 small carrot, grated

Fresh ground salt and pepper – to taste

1/2 Cup finely chopped onion

2 teaspoons chili powder

Directions:

Place all ingredients in a bowl, except flour. Stir well and gradually blend in flour. Stir until flour is well incorporated.

Preheat oven to 220C/450F and line baking sheet with parchment paper.

Form patties from prepared mixture and arrange onto baking sheet.

Bake for 10-12 minutes or until firm and nicely brown.

Serve with salad or salsa while still hot.

Tofu Stir Fry

Serves: 4

Ingredients:

14 oz. firm tofu, drained
5 oz. sliced button mushrooms
1 Cup sliced bell pepper
1 Cup carrot, cut into sticks
4 garlic cloves, thinly sliced
1/2 teaspoon crushed red pepper
1/2 teaspoon fresh ground salt
1 Cup broccoli florets
2 tablespoons pure olive oil
1/2 Cup finely chopped onions
1 teaspoon ginger

Directions:

Slice tofu into steaks and place in a bowl.
Drizzle over 1 tablespoon olive oil and add
ginger. Set aside for 15 minutes. Heat 1
tablespoon olive oil over medium-high heat
and add onions. Cook onions until soft. Add
tofu marinade, mushrooms and vegetables.
Cook, covered for 8-10 minutes or until
veggies are tender. Heat separate skillet over
medium-high heat and when hot, add tofu
steaks.

If needed add some more olive oil and cook tofu steaks until nicely golden-brown. Serve while still hot with vegetables on top.

White Bean-Quinoa Salad

Serves: 4

Ingredients:

2 Cups cooked quinoa

2 Cups cooked white beans

1 scallion, chopped

2 Tablespoons chopped fresh parsley

3 Tablespoons pure extra-virgin olive oil

1 red bell pepper, diced

Fresh ground salt and pepper – to taste

2 Tablespoons lemon juice

Directions:

In a large mixing bowl, combine quinoa, white beans, bell pepper, scallions and season with salt and pepper. In a small separate bowl, combine olive oil and lemon juice.
Drizzle over prepared salad and toss to combine. Serve immediately.

Yellow Split Pea Stew
Serves: 4
Ingredients:
2 cups water + 1 1/2 tablespoons, divided
3/4 Cup split yellow peas
1/2 Cup finely chopped carrots
1 large garlic clove, minced
1 1/2 Tablespoon olive oil
1/2-inch ginger, grated
3/4 teaspoon salt
1/4 teaspoon turmeric
1/2 small onion, chopped

Directions:
Place 2 cups water, carrots and peas in a medium sized sauce pan.
Heat over high heat and bring to boil. Reduce heat to medium and cook split peas until tender, for 30 minutes.
Meanwhile, heat olive oil in non-stick skillet. Add onions and cook for 5 minutes or until tender. Add garlic, turmeric and ginger; cook for 1 minute or until fragrant. Add remaining water, and stir; cover and cook for 3 minutes on low heat.
Add mixture to the cooked peas and stir well. Season additionally with salt and pepper.

NOTE: For more spice, replace ginger with hot sauce.

Rice and Beans
Serves: 4
Ingredients:
2 Cups brown rice, uncooked
15 oz. can red kidney beans, drained and rinsed
15 oz. can black beans, drained and rinsed
15 oz. can garbanzo beans, drained and rinsed
4 oz. can mild chilies, drained
1 Cup onion, chopped
14 oz. stewed tomatoes, drained
10 oz. green peas
1 Cup corn
Some pure olive oil
3 – 3 1/2 Cups water

Directions:
Preheat oven to 180C/350F. Heat some of the olive oil in a 5-quart cooking pot or Dutch oven over medium-high heat and add onion. Cook for 5 minutes or until tender. Add rice and stir while cooking until slightly opaque. Add tomatoes, beans, chilies and water. Bring mixture to boil over high heat. Cover tightly and place in the oven. Cook for 60 minutes or until liquid is absorbed and rice tender. Add

peas and corn and season according to desire. Place back in the oven to reheat. Serve while still hot.

Daniel Fast Dinner recipes

Mediterranean Couscous
Ingredients
1 Cup vegetable stock, preferably homemade
3/4 Cup whole wheat couscous, uncooked
1 small cucumber, unpeeled but properly washed, diced
1/8 teaspoon salt
3 medium tomatoes, diced and seeded
2 Tablespoons pure olive oil
2 Tablespoons lemon juice
4 medium green onions, chopped
1 Tablespoon chopped cilantro
Some crumbled tofu – if desired

Directions:
In a 2-quart sauce pan heat stock over high heat and bring to boil.
Stir in couscous and remove from the heat. Let it stand for 5 minutes.
In a large bowl, combine cucumber, tomatoes, onions and cilantro.
Add couscous. In small bowl, whisk olive oil, lemon juice and salt. Pour over prepared couscous and veggies. Toss to combine and serve.

Sweet Potato Burgers
Serves: 4
Ingredients:
1 1/2 Cups sweet potatoes, cooked with skin
1/4 Cup fresh corn
8 oz. black beans, drained and rinsed
1/2 teaspoon cumin
1/4 teaspoon chili powder
1/4 Cup chopped onion
3 Tablespoons rolled oats
1 Tablespoon sunflower seeds
1/4 teaspoon salt
1 garlic clove, minced
1/4 Cup cooked quinoa
1/2 teaspoon dried basil
1/2 Tablespoon olive oil

Directions:
Preheat oven to 180C/350F and line baking sheet with parchment paper. Mash half of the beans, but leave some chunks. Add in the rest of beans and stir to combine.
In a large bowl gently mash the sweet potatoes; stir in spices and dried basil. Add oats, corn, black beans, quinoa, sunflower seeds, garlic, onion and stir well to combine.

Form balls from the mixture and flatten to ½-inch thick patties. Arrange patties onto prepared baking sheet and bake in preheated oven for 15 minutes per side. Remove and serve with some fresh buns and fresh sliced avocado or peppers.

Red Lentil Curry

Serves: 4

Ingredients:

1 Cup red lentils

1/2 teaspoon chili powder

1/2 teaspoon ground cumin

1/2 teaspoon salt

1/2 teaspoon minced garlic

1/2 Tablespoon curry powder

1/2 teaspoon ground turmeric

1/2 Cup onion, chopped

1/2 Tablespoon vegetable oil

1 Tablespoon curry paste

1/2 teaspoon minced ginger

7 oz. tomato puree

Directions:

Wash lentils under cold water and place in a pot. Add enough water around 2 cups and heat over medium-high heat. Cover and bring lentils to simmer. Reduce heat to medium and simmer until tender. Add more water if necessary.

Meanwhile in a large skillet, heat oil. Add onions and cook over medium-low heat for 10 minutes or until caramelized. Combine curry paste, curry powder, and remaining spices in mixing bowl. When the onions are cooked add the curry mixture to the onions and cook over high heat, stirring constantly for 1-2 minutes. Stir in the tomato puree and reduce heat. Simmer until lentils are ready. Drain the lentils briefly and ad mix the curry base in. Serve while still hot garnished with fresh chopped cilantro.

Meatless "Meatballs"

Serves: 4

Ingredients:

1/4 Cup dried lentils

3/4 Cup water

1/4 teaspoon salt

1/4 teaspoon garlic

1 Tablespoon flax seeds meal

1 Tablespoon chopped walnuts

5 oz. frozen chopped spinach, thawed and pat dry

1/4 Cup brown rice flour

1/2 teaspoon dried basil

1 small garlic clove, minced

3/4 teaspoon olive oil

1/2 Cup sliced mushrooms

Directions:

Place lentils and water in medium sized sauce pan and bring to boil over high heat. Reduce heat to medium-low and add garlic and half of the onion. Cover and simmer for 40-45 minutes. Preheat oven to 180C/350F and brush baking tray with some olive oil.

Heat olive oil in skillet over medium heat and add spinach, mushrooms and remaining onion. Cook for 5 minutes stirring frequently.

When lentils are done, drain and add to the spinach mixture. Add rice flour, walnuts, basil and spices. Stir well and transfer into a food processor.

Blend for 10 seconds or until almost smooth. Form "meatballs" from the mixture and arrange onto prepared tray. Bake for 25-30 minutes. Set on wire rack to cool slightly before serving. Serve with fresh homemade tomato sauce.

Spring Quinoa

Serves: 4

Ingredients:

1/3 Cup quinoa

3/4 Cup water

Small pinch salt

1/3 Cup chopped asparagus

1/3 Cup chopped red bell peppers

1 1/2 Tablespoon pine nuts

1 small red onion, diced

1/3 Cup chopped tomatoes, seeded

1 Tablespoon chopped fresh parsley

1 garlic clove, minced

1/3 Tablespoon olive oil

1/2 teaspoon dried oregano

Directions:

Rinse quinoa and place in a sauce pan. Add water and bring to boil over high heat. Reduce heat to low and simmer for 20 minutes or until nearly all liquid is absorbed. Heat olive oil in non-stick skillet over medium-high heat. Add onion and cook for 5 minutes or until tender. Add garlic and cook further for 1 minute or until fragrant. Add remaining veggies and cook over low heat for 7 minutes. Add cooked quinoa to the skillet and stir in

parsley, pine nuts and oregano. Stir well and
serve while still hot.

Lettuce Wraps

Serves: 4

Ingredients:

1 Cup hummus

1/2 Cup sliced cucumber

8 romaine lettuce leaves

1/2 Cup zucchini, chopped

1/2 Cup shredded carrots

1 small bell pepper, sliced into thin stripes

Squeeze of fresh lemon or lime juice.

Directions:

Spread 2 tablespoon of hummus over lettuce leaves and sprinkle with a few drops of lemon juice. Top with carrots, cucumbers, zucchinis and pepper. Roll up like tortilla and serve.

Daniels Pizza
Serves: 4
Ingredients:
1 Cup warm water
2 1/2 Cups whole wheat flour
1 teaspoon salt
1 Tablespoon olive oil
2 Tablespoons flaxseed meal
1 Cup tomato sauce, homemade or canned with no sugar
1 onion, sliced into thin rounds
1 Cup sliced mushrooms
1 green bell pepper, sliced
1/2 Cup raw macadamia nuts

Directions:
Preheat oven to 220C/450F. Mix flour, salt, oil, flaxseeds and water in food processor. Pulse until dough forms. Turn dough onto floured surface and knead several times with hands. Roll the dough with floured rolling pin to 12-inch circle and place onto pizza stone or onto baking sheet sprinkled with some whole wheat flour.
Bake for 10 minutes and remove from the oven; set on wire rack. Spread tomato sauce on top of baked crust and top with

mushrooms, onion and bell pepper. Bake for 20 minutes and remove from oven. Meanwhile process macadamia nuts in food processor and sprinkle on top of prepared pizza. Slice and serve.

Rice and Tahini Cakes

Serves: 4

Ingredients:

1 Tablespoon tahini

1 1/2 Cups cooked brown rice

2 Tablespoons chopped spring onions

2 Tablespoons ground old fashioned oats

1 Tablespoon pure olive oil

1 teaspoon dried parsley

Directions:

Combine all ingredients, by order in a bowl.
Stir well.

Heat olive oil in large skillet over medium-high heat.

Form cakes from the prepared mixture, around 1/3 cup.

Cook for 5 minutes and carefully flip to other side. Cook further for 2 minutes.

Serve warm with fresh salad.

Daniel Fast Snacks

Toasted Almonds

Serves: 4

Ingredients:

1 Cup whole almonds

1/4 teaspoon cinnamon

1/8 teaspoon nutmeg

1/8 teaspoon salt

1/4 Tablespoon extra-virgin olive oil

Directions:

Preheat oven to 120C/250F and line baking tray with parchment paper.

Place almonds in a large bowl and drizzle with olive oil; toss to coat.

Add spices and shake until coated evenly.

Arrange almonds onto baking sheet in single layer and place in the oven.

Bake for 1 hour, stirring occasionally.

Serve when cooled or still slightly warm.

Raw Banana Sandwiches

Serves: 4

Ingredients:

1/4 Cup almond butter store bought all natural or homemade*

2 ripe bananas, large

1/4 teaspoon cinnamon

1 Tablespoon canned pumpkin, pureed

1/8 teaspoon vanilla, pure

1/8 teaspoon pumpkin pie spice

Directions:

Place almond butter, pumpkin and spices in a food processor; pulse until combined and creamy.

Peel bananas and slice into ½-inch rounds.

Top each banana slice with 1 teaspoon prepared butter and sandwich with another banana slice.

Sprinkle additionally with cinnamon and serve.

*To make homemade almond butter, mix 1 Cup roasted almonds with 1 teaspoon olive oil in a food processor. If mixture seems too dry add an additional 1 teaspoon of oil until right consistency.

Rice and Sesame Crackers

Serves: 4

Ingredients:

3/4 Cup brown rice flour

334 Cup wild rice cooked

1/4 Cup water

2 Tablespoons flax seeds meal, ground

3/4 teaspoon black sesame seeds

3/4 teaspoon white sesame seeds

1 1/2 Tablespoons extra-virgin olive oil

1 1/2 teaspoon salt

1/2 teaspoon cayenne pepper

Directions:

Preheat oven to 200C/400F and line baking tray with parchment paper.

Place rice flour, cooked rice, water, olive oil and spices in food processor. Pulse until ball starts to form. If mixture is too dry, add more water 1 Tablespoon at a time.

Transfer to the bowl and stir in sesame seeds, both, black and white.

Transfer the dough onto baking sheet, slightly oiled to prevent sticking. Press flat.

Cut out squares with a sharp knife.

Set the crackers onto baking tray and bake for 20 minutes.

Pumpkin Bars

Serves: 4

Ingredients:

1/2 Cup cooked pumpkin cubes

1/2 medium banana

1/2 teaspoon pumpkin pie spice

1/2 Tablespoon ground flaxseed meal

2 Tablespoons chopped walnuts

1 Tablespoon chopped dried cranberries

1/2 Cup almond meal

1/4 teaspoon grated orange zest

Directions:

Preheat oven to 180C/350F and line baking pan 4x2 inch with parchment paper.

Place pumpkin, banana, almond meal, cranberries, orange zest, pumpkin spice and ground flaxseeds meal in food processor.

Pulse until smooth.

Stir in walnuts and transfer the mixture into prepared baking pan.

Smooth the mixture flat with a spatula and bake in preheated oven for 40 minutes or until top is golden.

Set on wire rack to cool and slice into 8 bars.

Keep in airtight container wrapped in parchment paper.

Homemade Corn Tortilla Chips

Serves: 4

Ingredients:

1 Cup corn meal

1 1/2 Tablespoon lime juice

3/4 Cup warm water

1/2 teaspoon salt

1/8 teaspoon chili powder

1/4 teaspoon cumin

Directions:

Combine all ingredients in a bowl and stir until ball forms.

Let the dough rest for 15 minutes and meanwhile preheat the oven to 200C/400F.

Transfer the dough onto a half sheet or 9x13 ungreased baking pan and press with hands making it as thin as possible.

Cut with sharp knife into desired form and bake for 20 minutes.

Black Bean Hummus and Veggies

Serves: 4

Ingredients:

1 Tablespoon fresh lemon juice

8 oz. can beans, rinsed and drained

1 garlic clove, crushed

1/2 teaspoon ground cumin

1/4 teaspoon salt

1 Tablespoon sesame paste

1/8 teaspoon cayenne pepper

Vegetables by your choice – celery, carrot sticks

1-2 tablespoons water

Directions:

Place garlic in food processor and add beans, lemon juice, spices and sesame paste. Process until smooth; add enough water, 1 tablespoon at the time, to reach desired consistency, pulsing after each addition. Serve with vegetables of your choice.

Sweet Potato Chips

Serves: 2

Ingredients:

2 sweet potatoes, medium
1/2 teaspoon chili powder
2 Tablespoons pure olive oil
1/2 teaspoon salt
1/2 teaspoon smoked paprika
1/4 teaspoon nutmeg

Directions:

Preheat oven to 200C/400F and line baking tray with parchment paper.

Mix all spices in a small bowl. Wash and scrub sweet potatoes and using a mandolin cutter or food processor slicer cut thin slices. Transfer sweet potatoes in a bowl and add olive oil; toss to coat well. Add spice mix and toss and shake until coated evenly. Arrange potatoes onto baking sheet in single layer.

Bake for 20 minutes, flipping them after 10 minutes. Set on wire rack to cool to room temperature and serve.

Fruity Cookies

Serves: 20 balls

Ingredients:

1 Cup mashed bananas
1 Cup finely grated apple
1 1/2 Cup oats
3/4 Cup frozen raspberries
1/2 Cup dried cranberries
1 teaspoon ground cinnamon
Small pinch salt
1/2 Cup walnuts, chopped

Directions:

Combine mashed bananas and apple in a bowl. Add rolled oats and stir to combine. Add cranberries, cinnamon, walnuts and salt; mix well.

Add the raspberries and stir until combined. Preheat oven to 180C/350F and line baking tray with parchment paper.

Form dough into small balls. Place onto baking sheet and bake in preheated oven for 15-20 minutes. Set on wire rack to cool and serve. Keep in airtight container.

Slow Cooker Daniel Fast Recipes

Chickpea Stew

Serves: 4

Ingredients:

1 Cup water

1/2 teaspoon pure olive oil

1 medium potato, peeled and diced

1/2 Tablespoon mild curry

1/2 Tablespoon grated ginger

8 oz. can chickpeas, drained and rinsed

1 garlic clove, minced

1 red bell pepper, diced

14 oz. can tomatoes, with juices

1/2 Cup coconut milk

1/8 teaspoon salt

1 Cup cauliflower, chopped florets

1/2 Cup finely diced onion

Directions:

Heat olive oil in skillet over medium-high heat. Add onion and cook until tender, for 5 minutes. Add potato and salt; cook for 3-4 minutes. Stir in curry, ginger and garlic; cook for 40 seconds. Pour 1/4 cup vegetable stock and scrape the bottom of pan to deglaze and transfer the content in slow cooker. Add remaining ingredients, except coconut milk and stir to combine. Cover and cook for 4 hours on high. In the last 15 minutes of cooking stir in coconut milk.

Cover and continue cooking for remaining 15 minutes. Adjust seasoning and serve while still hot.

Quinoa Crock Pot Stew

Serves: 4

Ingredients:

14 oz. can diced tomatoes

1 green bell pepper, diced

1/2 dried chipotle pepper

1 teaspoon chili powder

1/2 Cup uncooked quinoa

1 garlic clove, crushed

3 1/2 Cups water

Fresh ground salt and pepper

1/2 teaspoon coriander powder

1/2 teaspoon cinnamon

1 Tablespoon fresh cilantro chopped

1/2 onion, diced

1/2 lb. dried black beans, rinsed

Directions:

Place all ingredients, except salt in a slow cooker.

Cook on high for 5 hours or until black beans are tender.

Add the salt and stir to combine. Remove the chipotle before serving and if desired, serve with lime wedges.

Squash and Coconut Curry

Serves: 4

Ingredients:

1/2 Cup onion, diced

1 garlic clove, minced

1 tomato, diced

1 1/2 Cup water

7 oz. coconut milk

3/4 Cup peas

1 1/2 Tablespoon mild curry

3/4 Cup chickpeas, dried and rinsed

1 1/4 Cup butternut squash, peeled and cubed into 1-inch cubes

1/2 Cup chopped kale

1/2 teaspoon salt

1 Tablespoon chopped cilantro

Directions:

Add all ingredients in slow cooker, except kale and peas.

Stir well, cover and cook on high for 6 hours. Around 30 minutes before serving add in the fresh peas and kale.

Stir and continue cooking for an additional 30 minutes. If desired, serve hot with brown rice and garnish with cilantro.

Slow Cooker Ratatouille

Serves: 6

Ingredients:

4 small zucchinis, sliced into rounds

2 garlic cloves, crushed

2 onions, sliced into rounds

2 green bell peppers, sliced into strips

2 large tomatoes, chopped

2 teaspoons salt

 6 oz. tomato puree

1 Tablespoon fresh basil, chopped

1 Tablespoon fresh oregano, chopped

1/4 Cup fresh parsley

1/4 Cup olive oil

1/2 teaspoon fresh ground pepper

1 eggplant, sliced into rounds

Directions:

Slice all veggies into 1/4-inch thin rounds and peppers in strips.

Arrange veggies in slow cooker in following order; half of onions, half of eggplants, half of zucchinis, half of garlic, half of green pepper, half of tomatoes, half of herbs and half of tomato puree. Repeat layer and drizzle with olive oil. Cover and cook on low for 8 hours. Serve while still hot.

Cabbage Soup

Serves: 4

Ingredients:

1/2 head green cabbage, cored and sliced

1/4 Cup pure olive oil

2 garlic cloves

1 carrot, chopped into ½-inch pieces

1 Cup green beans, cut into ½-inch pieces

1 small red bell pepper

7 oz. pureed tomatoes

1-quart water

2 celery stalks, chopped

1/2 Cup onion, copped

1/2 Cup cooked brown rice

1 teaspoon dried basil

1 teaspoon dried oregano

Fresh ground salt and pepper – to taste

Directions:

Place veggies, spices and rice in slow cooker. Add water, rice, olive oil and stir well. Cover and cook on low for 6 hours. Serve while still hot.

Bean and Spinach Enchiladas

Serves: 4

Ingredients:

1 Cup frozen corn

10 oz. chopped spinach

15 oz. black beans, rinsed and drained

1/2 teaspoon ground cumin

6 Cups chopped lettuce

1/2 Cup grape tomatoes, halved

1/2 cucumber, halved and sliced

3 Tablespoons lime juice, fresh

2 Tablespoons olive oil

3 Cups salsa

8 corn tortillas

1/2 Cup cashew halves - -processed in food blender for 15 seconds

Directions:

In a medium bowl mash half of the beans. Add cumin, spinach, corn, 1/4 cup processed cashews, remaining beans, salt and pepper; stir to combine. Spread 1 cup salsa in the bottom of 4-quart slow cooker.

Divide bean mixture evenly between corn tortillas and place them seam side down on top of salsa and pour over remaining salsa and cashews.

Cover and cook on low for 3 hours. Combine lettuce, lime juice, olive oil, salt and pepper in a bowl; toss to combine. Serve whit prepared enchiladas.

Vegetarian Goulash

Serves: 6

Ingredients:

4 tomatoes, cut into wedges

3 garlic cloves, chopped

1 jalapeno pepper, diced

1/2 bunch parsley, chopped

1 Tablespoon smoked paprika

2 onions, sliced into half moons

2 bay leaves

1 lb. green beans, trimmed and chopped into ½-inch pieces

1 Cup corn

1/2 lb. elbow whole wheat pasta

4 Cups water

4 Tablespoon vinegar

2 green bell peppers, chopped

2 red bell peppers, chopped

Salt and pepper – to taste

Directions:

Place spices, water, veggies and vinegar in a slow cooker. Cover and cook on low for 6 hours. In last 30 minutes of cooking stir in the elbow pasta and remove bay leaves.

Continue cooking and serve while still hot.

Barley Vegetable Soup

Serves: 4

Ingredients:

1 medium celery stalk, chopped
1/2 Cup uncooked barley
1/4 teaspoon fennel seeds, optional
3/4 Cup green beans
3./4 Cup frozen corn
7 oz. vegetable homemade stock
3 Cups water
7 oz. can tomatoes
2 garlic cloves crushed
1/4 Cup chopped basil
3/4 Cup carrots, sliced
1/4 Cup chopped onion
1/4 Cup chopped red bell pepper

Directions:

In a 4-quart slow cooker place all ingredients, except tomatoes making sure that carrots are the first layer. Cover and cook on low for 6-8 hours.
10 minutes before serving, stir in the tomatoes. Cover and continue cooking for 10 minutes. Serve while still hot.

Daniel Fast Smoothies

Sunny Smoothie

Serves: 1

Ingredients:

1/4 Cup strawberries

1/4 Cup peaches, chopped

1/4 Cup pineapple chunks

1 banana, ripe

3 Tablespoons fresh orange juice

Directions:

Place all ingredients in blender and blend until smooth.

Serve with ice cubes, if desired.

Oat and Banana Smoothie

Serves: 1

Ingredients:

1/4 Cup almonds

1 Cup almond milk

1 banana, sliced

1/2 Cup halved strawberries

1/2 Cup rolled oats

Directions:

Place all ingredients in blender and pulse until smooth. Serve immediately.

Mango Coconut Smoothie

Serves: 2

Ingredients:

1 Cup coconut milk
2 Cups mango chunks
Few ice cubes
1/4 teaspoon ground cinnamon
Juice for 1/2 lime

Directions:

Place milk, cinnamon, ice cubes and lime juice
in food processor.
Blend until smooth. Add mango and continue
blending until well combined and smooth.
Serve immediately.

Pear Avocado Smoothie

Serves: 2

Ingredients:

1/2 Cup pear juice

1/4 Cup silken tofu, drained

3 oz. avocado, peeled

1 Cup ice

Directions:

Process all ingredients except ice until smooth. Add ice and blend until smooth and well combined. Serve immediately.

Pomegranate Smoothie

Serves: 2

Ingredients:

1/4 Cup coconut milk

1 Cup pomegranate seeds

1 Cup baby spinach

1 Tablespoon chia seeds

2-3 strawberries, halved

Directions:

Place all ingredients in food processor and pulse until smooth.

Serve immediately and garnish with pomegranate seeds, if desired.

Melon Almond Smoothie
Serves: 2
Ingredients:
2 Cups melon, peeled and diced
2 Cups chilled almond milk
1/4 teaspoon grated ginger, fresh

Directions:
Place all ingredients in food processor and pulse until smooth.
Serve immediately.

Kiwi Avocado Smoothie

Serves: 1

Ingredients:

2 kiwis, peeled and chopped
1/4 Cup soy or coconut milk
3 ice cubes
1/2 large avocado, peeled

Directions:

Place all ingredients in food processor and
pulse; start on low speed, increasing to high.
Blend until smooth and creamy.
Serve immediately.

Berry Apple Smoothie

Serves: 2

Ingredients:

1 apple, peeled and cored

1 ripe banana, peeled

1 Cup fresh raspberries

1 Cup almond milk

1 Cup ice

1 juicy pear, peeled and chopped

Directions:

Place all ingredients in food processor.

Blend until smooth.

Serve immediately.

Daniel Fast Desserts

Frozen Banana Bars

Serves: 12

Ingredients:

1 Cup chopped cashews

1 Cup chopped dates

1 teaspoon cinnamon

1/4 teaspoon nutmeg

1/2 teaspoon grated orange zest

2 Cups sliced bananas about 2 bananas

Directions:

Place all ingredients in food processor and pulse until smooth.

Transfer to 8x8-inch baking dish lined with parchment paper.

Freeze for 3 hours or until firm.

Serve immediately.

Mango Sorbet

Serves: 2

Ingredients:

2 Cups mango chunks, frozen
2 Tablespoons orange juice
1 Tablespoon pear or pineapple juice

Directions:

Place all ingredients in food processor and pulse until smooth.
Scoop into bowls and serve immediately.

Fig and Rice Pudding

Serves: 2

Ingredients:

1 Cup coconut milk

2 figs, ripe

1 teaspoon cinnamon

1 Cup brown rice, cooked

Directions:

Place coconut milk in small sauce pan and whisk well.

Heat over medium heat and bring to a simmer.

Add rice, 1/2 teaspoon cinnamon and figs and continue simmering for 5-7 minutes or until mixture starts to thicken.

Spoon into bowls and sprinkle with remaining cinnamon.

Berry Frozen Yogurt

Serves: 3-4

Ingredients:

1 Cup frozen strawberries
1 Cup frozen raspberries, blackberries or blueberries
1/2 Cup almond milk kefir
1 frozen banana, chunked

Directions:

Place all ingredients in food processor.
Pulse until smooth and freeze for 1 hour.
Serve garnished with fresh berries, if desired.

Fruity Oats Cookies

Serves: 12

Ingredients:

1 Cup unsweetened apple sauce
2 large bananas, mashed
1 teaspoon cinnamon
1/4 teaspoon salt
1/2 Cup dried apricots, chopped
1/4 Cup chopped almonds
1 1/2 Cups rolled oats
1 Cup finely chopped strawberries

Directions:

Preheat oven to 180C/350F and line baking tray with parchment paper.
Combine apple sauce and mashed bananas; stir in almonds and fruits, dried and fresh.
Add cinnamon and rolled oats; stir until combined.
Scoop 1/4 cup spoonfuls to baking sheet and flatten each dollop to 1/2-inch thick.
Bake for 30 minutes or until golden brown.
Set on wire rack to cool before serving and keep in airtight container.

Blueberry Muffins

Serves: 12

Ingredients:

3 ripe bananas, mashed
2 1/4 Cups almond flour
1/4 teaspoon salt
1 teaspoon ground flax seeds
2 Tablespoons melted coconut oil
1/2 vanilla pod, seeds scraped out
1 Cup frozen blueberries

Directions:

Preheat oven to 180C/350F and line 12-hole muffin tin with paper cases.

Combine oil and vanilla in a bowl. Gradually add in almond flour, flax seeds and salt; stir until just combined. Fold in blueberries and scoop the batter into paper cups to 2/3 full. Bake for 25-30 minutes or until firm to the touch. Let cool and serve.

Banana Pop Bites

Serves: 4

Ingredients:

2 bananas

1 can coconut milk – refrigerated overnight, milk removed cream reserved

1/2 teaspoon pure vanilla

1/2 Cup ground almonds

Directions:

Slice bananas into 1-inch pieces.

Line large plate with baking paper and set aside.

In a bowl, combine coconut cream with vanilla; whisk using electric whisk until fluffy.

Dip bananas in prepared cream and arrange onto lined plate; sprinkle with ground almonds and set in freezer until firm.

Serve and enjoy.

Raspberry Crunchy Bars

Serves: 12 bars

Ingredients:

1 Cup whole wheat flour

1 Cup rolled oats

1 teaspoon ground flax seeds

1/2 Cup coconut or almond butter, softened

1 1/4 Cup raspberries

1 Tablespoon orange juice

Directions:

Place raspberries in a sauce pan and add orange juice. Mash with fork and heat over medium-high heat.

Cook for 10 minutes or until thick and mixture resembles jam. Remove from the heat and set aside.

In a medium sized bowl, combine flour, flaxseeds and rolled oats.

Add coconut butter and with fingers stir in rolled oats mixture, until evenly moistened.

Transfer 2 Cup mixture into 8x8-inch baking pan lined with parchment paper.

Spread raspberry jam in an even layer and sprinkle with remaining rolled oats.

Bake for 35-38 minutes or until golden brown. Set on wire rack to cool before slicing.

Made in the USA
Monee, IL
19 February 2022

91458120R10056